Rainbow Elephant

Rebecca Barrett,
Thank you for
the support!
I appreciate it. ☺
Enjoy your read.
Taria Person
"The Realest
Person" 2019

Rainbow Elephant

By

Taria Person
Old and new poems

This book is dedicated to: **my love**, Chanel Braswell; **my sisters,** Tamika Person and Mikaya White; and **my friends**, Miah Welch (Rose), Daniel J. Grimes, and Alex Brooks.

Contents

Acknowledgements

I am immensely appreciative of the love, support, and mentorship that I have received from Patricia Jones, Marquez Rhyne, my poetry mom: Rhea Carmon, and my UT Moms: Margaret Lazarus Dean and Katy Chiles. Big thanks to Chris Barton, Megan Leanne Smith, and Jonathan (Courageous) Clark for friendship and several workshops, my Knoxville Poetry Slam family and Southern Fried Poetry Slam family, fellow cohorts from Ridgeway, and Treasure Hightower and Stan Johnson from SEEED. There's much gratitude to <u>every-single-person</u> who has ever supported me, and/or given me words of encouragement to rise higher. Much love. Peace.

Preface

At 6:30 AM, I was sipping homemade lemon, ginger, and mint tea from a travel mug, and waiting for my shift to begin at Rainbow Child Care Center. I remember sitting at my desk, battling through little kid germs, and juggling ideas of unworthiness and frustration around in the empty space. My desk was a small table located in the back of the classroom, which sat next to the arts & crafts area, the reading station, and a shelf full of puzzles and scattered toys.

A deluge of pre-school students ran in, holding up their breakfasts—a boxed-milk, cereal in a cup, and an apple, all in a clear sack—like a child uplifting a new goldfish. A few of them disposed of their food as they entered then proceeded to crisscross-apple-sauce onto the learning rug, in order to wait for the main teacher to arrive. Squatting to the ground with an arm stretched, my face livened with a smile that showed every pearly tooth. "Good morning, students! Good morning. Alright…alright, let's find our seats," I responded, rising to sip some tea. Several of them proceeded to hug me anyway, rushing to put their backpacks onto their hooks, afterwards.

Eventually, the main teacher—a woman wearing a ponytail with bangs, a red shirt with a Rainbow Child Care logo on it, and a nametag that read, "Mrs. Upton"—waddled in with an open coat, and a purse and fast food bag clenched into her fists.

"Sorry, I'm late. Georgia's traffic is absolutely terrible and people can't drive. You would think that I would be used to it by now," she explained.

"It's no problem. It's all good. You're here now," I responded.

The students sat on the learning rug, talking and laughing amongst themselves. Mrs. Upton bellowed, blowing her bangs from her forehead.

"Ok. Have you ever taught a lesson before? I mean it's not rocket science, so it should be simple."

The roll in her eyes let me know that she *knew* I was inexperienced.

A student ran to my side and yanked at my jacket sleeve for undivided attention.

"Go sit down!" Mrs. Upton yelled. She attempted to rip his arm from me, and almost from his body. He ran back to the rug. I smiled at him, waiting for his response.

I looked into the teacher's brown, drifting eyes and answered, "Yeah, of course I've taught a lesson before."

"Thank God," Mrs. Upton said sarcastically. "They always put me with somebody who *thinks* they know something, but they usually, really don't," she replied, and piled a stack of papers into the palm of my hand. I sipped tea and read the directions.

The teacher announced, "Alright class! You should be looking at me, and you should be on a voice level—BE quiet! We have...um."

"Ms. T," I reminded her.

"Right. Anyways, Ms. T, she's fairly new. She doesn't know what's going on here. So don't you even dare think about acting up because we have company…understood?" Collectively, the students filled the room with an extended, "Yesssss, Mrs. Uptonnnnnnn!"

The teacher directed her gaze back to me, and continued, "All you have do, is get them to draw a picture and complete the sentence: 'I want to be (blank) when I grow up.' That's all. You don't have to read it."

"Thank you. I got it," I expressed, continuing to read. The students stared up from the learning rug with engaged, glossy eyes.

Each sheet had a box for drawing, a word bank full of cookie cutter professions, and a sentence with a font size that was as big as the ones on the beginner handwriting worksheets. I gathered half of the students, assisting them to the chair with their names on the back. The other half remained on the carpet with the teacher, while she ate French fries, and read some adaptation of "The Three Little Pigs".

At the activity/learning tables, I was trying to guide students the way that the teacher insisted. I placed my tea on my desk, rolled my sleeves up, and placed the assignment before each of them.

Thank God? How hard is it for me—an artist, a writer, a teacher, an employee at a childcare center—to instruct students on drawing a picture and writing a sentence?

The teacher's eyes bounced to me from the rug. She projected, "I'll huff and I'll puff," in the background; however, reminded me that they only needed a small piece of paper. I asked the students if they wanted to draw a small picture or a large picture, before I asked what color crayon they wanted. I took one of the activity-chairs from another table to join them.

"What's up, Ms. T?" Chris asked.

"What's good?" I responded. The student held up his drawing on a sheet of paper, which was as big as he was. I continued, "Wow! Awesome. Alright...now express to me—"

"They don't know what the word express means. Don't confuse them! Use basic words," Mrs. Upton interjected.

"Both of my mommies say that word all the time, and one has a bowtie like you too, Ms. T," the student said.

"That's so amazing!" I exclaimed, asking the rest of the students if they knew what the word "Express," meant. The students all nodded, but I gave the definition anyway, to avoid confusion.

"Express in a drawing and in a sentence, what it is that you will be when you grow up," I asked.

Chris rushed to his seat, wrote and talked amongst his peers.

"Ms. T! Ms. T! Chris said a bad word!" Kevin fell over his friends to get to me.

"What did he say?" I asked.

"He said...he said, um, that he got two mamas, and my

mama said that was a bad word!"

"Well, him saying that he has two mommies isn't a bad word," I said.

"Yeah it is! You can't have two mamas. I have a mama and a daddy," he announced.

"So Kevin, let me make sure I'm getting the picture clear, because you have a mama and daddy, that means, Chris doesn't have two mommies?" I asked.

Kevin stood quietly, glaring at me. I joined in on the staring contest, and was surprised that it had lasted for about fifteen seconds due to my question. Soon after, he walked back to his friends, with his mouth open like he was thinking seriously about something.

Sarah walked up next in her Spider-man shirt, and pink shoes that lit up with each step.

"Magnificent! I think I know who you want to be based on your picture, but express to me who you are going to be?" I said.

"Spiderman!" She exclaimed then shot an imaginary web at me. I jumped out of the way pretending I was almost hit. Students laughed, smiled, and imitated her action out of their seats. Mrs. Upton stared at me like she wanted to say something, but just sat with her mouth ajar and with a fixed glare.

"Scholars…it's great to be excited and have fun, but we have an assignment to complete," I reminded them. "Find your seat and put a bubble in your mouth."

The students blew up their cheeks like they were playing a trumpet. Many switched crayon colors to really get focused.

"Now, how are you going to achieve your mission?" I asked Sarah. She shot at me again, smiled, and ran to the table without saying a word.

Damion displayed a scruffy ninja. Students snickered and scribbled on the backs of their assignment.

"I like it! Is it a ninja?" I asked.

"How you know?" He gasped.

"It looks like a ninja to me."

"When I'm...I'm growed up. Imma be fighting everything like a ninja! Watch." Damion said, as he kicked and fought the air.

"To be a ninja, doesn't always mean to fight, young grasshopper," I said, striking a pose with him.

"What?" Damion asked.

"You can love!" Chris shouted.

Chris and Sarah jumped up and hugged me.

"Now Chris, express to me who you are, based on your drawing and sentence."

Chris handed me his sheet of paper. My eyes shifted between the vibrant lines and swirls. *Ha. This is so me, a vortex of some sort.*

"Ms. T, I drew it for you," he said.

The picture was every color of a rainbow, with one single black crayon mark, funneling through the center.

"This is so beautiful. You're so incredible and courteous. Thank you for sharing your art with me."

"Do you know what it is?" He asked with a grin on his face.

My eyes connected with his and I shook my head in honesty.

"Not exactly. What is it?"

"Ms. T, it's a Rainbow Elephant!"

Mother

My eyes speak phrases like, 'Mama,
I remember when you used to love me'
down the valleys of my face, where hilltops
smudged rouge used to remain high
from your embrace.
Now, I can't even hug you without it being gay.
Like my eyes are fixed on the female physique
not caring about who it is?
Like I'm interested in the bodies of little girls
and could even think about taking advantage
of a little kid?

Me and my sisters,
can't even sit in the same room without you asking,
'Hey! What y'all in there doing?'
Like I'm hammering images
of what "Gay" is into their brains,
screwing up the family house. I always wondered...
Why my door had to be open, especially when
I had guests?
Because you always guessed that my friends were my girlfriends
but deep down, my girlfriend is only recognized as my friend
I'm confused.

Smashed inside your box of paradoxes.

Mind absent from my body.
Heart not allowed to fall
in the palms of love, if it's not a male;
I might as well hold my breath and pass
out of these tests that I never get:
a good job, excellent or a sticker on
just a reminder that, "You need a man!
I don't care if he's no good,

1

as long as you put this stick on her."
Me.

You are constant Michael Meyer slices
in my vertebrae for no reason
other than to kill my esteem
with your sharp phrases like:

"You too pretty to be gay,
I don't know what you want me to say,
I don't speak 'gay'.
When you gone get out of this little tomboy phase?
Oh my God, Taria this is not real love!"

But you love me?

And I know you know what real love is.
Just unravel your thoughts
from the left and right atrium
left and right ventricle, to hear
the rhythmic message that your heart
is trying to get you to understand.
And I will never understand
why love has to be something
that society accepts? Exceptions
on my love, to make them feel
comfortable.
Feet propped up
on the backs of minorities.

And Mama...

I thought that you would know
how it feels to be bashed
for no reason. Treasonous.

Life sucked out of you
"A Raisin in the Sun."
Massa screaming, 'nigger'
this, nigger' that
when you don't even consider yourself one.
Same thing for the word 'dyke.'
The walls where eyelashes remain
prostrate, are not strong enough
to seize flooding.

So it's wrong for you
to even fix your lips
to let the word, 'dyke' slip
out of your mouth

I feel like a motherless child.
Sometimes.
A one-year-old child, with a lot of shit
on my back and you have neglected me.
A long way from home,
since the day that you put me out,
and I've been crawling
on this crooked line. Walking around
with a lot of shit on my mind,
and I've been wanting to ask you this
for a very long time…

How does it feel, to know that…I still love you?

Loving me is Wrong?
I remember when I was innocent
opinions could not touch me.
My private parts
roamed past walls
and felt safe.

An unflinching personality,
like when I was five and possessive
about all of my dreams,
a box of poems flooded with images.
I wrote on canvases in the basement.
Back at home, all I did was lie
on pallets.
Cocooned into haunted generational
situations reminding me
that I was born

in a paradoxical atmosphere.
Guilt slips through my poetry
like birds crying in the morning
when many people ain't listening.

A rusted title like myself
on a shelf next to Bradbury or Poe.
I'm trying not to censor
my tuneful exclamations
in the corner
of the library drinking tea.
Attempting to reason with my logic.
I'm screaming out,
'Montresor' or 'Jesus' in the closet.

Trying not to hang or linger
like the finger of a grandmother telling me

right from wrong,
wrong herself,
fabricated in a different form;
but still, I sit
and sip away from irony or drama
within the Realest Person.

Same day, I meta-person.
An apostrophe cultured in unfinished expressions,
things that I cannot hear, but are rehearsed.
I'm just talking.
Thinking about dying nine ways
on life ten trying to find life in tin cans,
nowadays, I'm numb on the kitchen floor
heart unconscious on the ceiling.
Knocking on wood:
am I living? am I living? am I living,
yet?

I'm the subject of abject turned object.
Delved into too many tears
only getting my feet wet.
An abomination of stationary shards,
too sentimental,
a legendary hegemony
unmanageable cuticles from the hands of discourse,
scrapping at wet nightmares.
Stuck on streets full of elm trees trying to breathe.

Beware.

Structures color my lips purple,
sandwiched perception:
the blood and the blues.
A drinking, thinking,

smoking, swaying transcendental
blunt of identity in the exhaust
of an entity's purity
for me and against me.
A sacrificial possibility from back in the day
obsessed with *Reading Rainbow.*

Now, I'm just a nigga reading books
an agenda-ed lesbo.
Three shots to the chest
a moon burned slow
or star night light in a wall
trying to escape
being haunted by the sublime.

If loving me is wrong, I don't want to *be.*

Like My Great-Granddaddy Raising the Sun at 5,
I'm dreaming about clouds
splitting the sky wide
pouring in flavor
like a faucet dripping
water offbeat
into trees
or the ground vibrating
rhythm
allowing leaves to dance
giving air color
a name
or rhyme
time to breathe

I wake to morning skies
like scriptures
creating prayers
after a long day of listening
to space
smear smiles into mountains
rising like his hair
a snow white-top
speckled with summertime
or cobwebs from apple trees

Dipped in Black
Black hands
Black lips
fingertips that scare
Black
Brown
Blonde hair
Straight, the only way in their eyes

SURPRISE!

The revolution, can be purchased online
in an eBook   look…
Brown swisher, green reef,
pose as halo

High to heaven. High after 7 pm.
Tylenol to go with that **Black** lung
Black sung. O' **Black** sung,
but **Black** still sings.
It "Rings around the Rosie" and falls
in love.

Pocket full of notes
chokes up, eyes closed, gulps hard
my God
is looking through **Black** holes
cavities   crevices to find

Black love, **Black** love,
Black love, **Black** love   and appreciation
Black tears
Black tears are still clear
lately, just a reflection of **Black** face
on repeat

repeat after me
I mean them
ventriloquist holding up poison

Poison control! Poison control!

Controlling amber skinned babies
to fall from weeping willows
like cheap pillows
stiff and hard fossilized resin
in the sun
stain with the sun
refrain,   from the sun
you may become too Beautiful

too Full, too Light
Powerful
High
Close like a bad bee swarming around face
to find place

Lost
areola in bra, out of bra
Honey
stains like Coca-Cola
deteriorating follicle to shoulder
enjoyable

losing Power once cracked open
we were cracked open   cracked open and can't move
for a long time
without going back like we left something
patting pockets for change
bills, skills, keys to open up
eyes to open up

skies

We act like we can't reach into **Black** hole
and deliver
reach in and pull out rabbit
scared of the vibrations
scared to use tongue as navigation
to overcome

Boy, the temptation
Girl, never woman, only hoe
born in Eden
professional at growing
We create!
Can't look pass figure
8 times in the mirror
makes plate full of:
depression
stress
insecurities

segregate   segregate

can't have my jealousy touching
my self hate

that's too close, too real, too many judges
against one mental
one pencil   sketching out rainbows
in college rule

at the end of that spectrum
rain clouds pour in diversity

but we say

you can't be Different
can't be the Same
Speaking
Silent
Marching. Nonviolent.

Can't be taking rain clouds   and squeezing
like sponges
dripping Color
can't wonder   only worry
about today   not the past
so the past can haunt and spread
like wild fire signaling another life lost
blunt

our bodies wrapped in rainbow
along the shoulders like shawl,
but go ahead and lay down
and finish enjoying your nightmare
Dipped in **Black**

Butterflies

Caterpillar
waiting to be self
squirming out of skin
daring to be beautiful
wants to find strength
to remain elevated
but scared to develop color

Essence of a Woman
Past the cover
there was boldness
words fell to etch and sketch
themselves onto wrists
bleeding into the beds of her toe nails
head up
she died to be born again
giving birth to styles
spritzed up like a bow tie
she's an up-do
perfect image of a statue
wearing haikus on her hips
(that's where the switch comes from)
her form is free verse
meta-discursive
a world that stands on earth
important
importing tracks—sounds, beats,
rhythm to speech
the soul was conceived in the belly of her tongue
speak up

Genesis is not the beginning of her story

On the Third Day she Rose
I woke up as mist
light and ready
free and wild like life in the Serengeti
I'm spaghetti on a Tuesday night
demanding my bread
and fish, I've fed nations
standing behind me
do you see
these mountains?
Do you see these wings?
as I "Bankhead Bounce"
and fling haters under locs that rain out
these fountains cleanse
my body sheds
daily rebuilding
an ocean of emotions
coasting
do you feel this filling enter you?

I woke up a fist
hitting the chest of oppression,
do you hear
the beat? Or the feet of black souls
and white hands dance
down the streets of Jefferson
in Nashville, TN
where I raised
in the garden
they slaved
I'm marching
I overcame a long time ago
you can't stand me
I subzero toes like cement
make women and men

shake their pupils around this figure
eight and pigment I'm full as fros.
Do you hear those black clouds
echo?
Blasphemous is what they call me
I laugh and curse
to defend my purpose
I'm me
on purpose

I woke up a kiss
on the spine of love at dusk
in my nature carrying
a full lip is normal
spraying similes like smiles
exalting sublime taste
robust mind and face that, "bangs
like bomb" that goes **Black**
powerful
I'm a tower full of dandelions growling
I don't follow rules
I'm a muse that sizzles
pops jitter on taste buds
slightly effervescent
bold and demanding
I am presence
fermented paper folded
wise with space
created to create

I woke up a God

Brick House
I remember when I was transformed
made of brick
dick stacked on top of me
and hickies vandalized my foundation.
Brick, dick, spit everywhere, looking
hands mounted on the carpet
cement and semen flows through
the crevices. My palms.
There's nothing I can't handle.

Handle, escape, run.
"She's just playing. She's just drunk."
Hide.
"Go get her...go get her."
You can read me, sometimes,
I'm not stationary.
I spaghetti onto the kitchen floor.
Brick, dick, spit every where, looking
swaying. Leaving. No staying
not at a standstill.
"Let's just go back to the room."

Running, touching, bumping handle.
There's nothing I can't handle.
Don't let this exterior fool.
"Don't worry we got you."
Black, dick, spit handle
door dismantled. My room, my bed
inside, decor and pain peels.
Flashes, not able to feel.
See, pain pills flow through walls.
My spirit has left me. I think she's in the hall now
running, escaping, *twist the handle.* "Close the door."

Brain on floor. Feet leave ground
floating, still standing.
Pretty tough, right?
Nothing I can't handle.
Pretty solid. Pretty sturdy.
Don't worry about me. Falling.
Handle. I have the handle now
and I'm standing like objects
that have left their foundation in the cabinet.
Unreachable. Don't look. Don't touch.

"Come here. Give him kiss. Now me.
His name is Tyrone"
Wait...that's my daddy's name. Daddy,
are you here to save me?
Someone.
Just don't look. Don't touch. It hurts
when the front door is open.
The front door while open, has a gush of wind
that roars like flowers. "Do you love me.
You love me?" Not
to the beat of every piece dropping.

The entire time, not a sound, lips captive
speech plucked like petals
words fall with power.
Brick, dick, flashes. Can't see.
Swaying. Leaving. Falling now. Crawling.
How can I get to the other side of the room?
Hide.
They're leaving. No, staying. Tyrone is back
I'm praying.

My soul is standing outside. Listening.
"Hands up." Shirt off. Witnessing me.

"I can smell you."
Pay attention to the signs. Don't speed pass.
Stop rushing, trying to force yourself
inside. No room for you to slide in.
Brick. Sticks and stones thrown
add structure. No words can blow me down.
You can't blow me down.
"Get down. Hike up."
But...
"Lesbians like head, right?
Brick, dick, spit.
"Aw shit."

Cement flows through crevices.
Palms hold sign that reads,
'Don't let my exterior fool you.
Stationary, inside, walls beat up. Still standing
Pretty
Beautiful
Nothing I can't handle

Fuh Color'd Clo'es

Gotta lil dye lef in ma wangs
col' showas don't get meh clean
an' bubba baffs in yessirdays
don't fade meh nun, I'm alive
wen yah leave me on de flo'
walk'n in yah room wid alla dem clo'es

Yah gotta fo'd dem nannies unda yah clo'es
widout meh. Der's suppo't in ma wangs
ma straps, so why I'm on the flo'?
Lika collectable…ain't I still clean?
Do yah blo' durst offameh tuh make meh live?
Nawl, yah stepp'd owt wondafuh yessirday

An' yessirday, I wuz real wen yah wuz fabricat'd
livin' in dah a'justments of ma arms. Ma cloe's.
I suck powda inta deeze cups, namin' dem alive.
Livin' on dis dam' flo'…ma wangs…
kinda clean.
I flew gracefuh…lika lady. You see me on da flo'?

Flo'ridin' on a'fro'd carpet, cuz yah don't need meh no mo'.
Yessirday, I 'member makin' yah perk in dem shirts
cleanin' yah mess. Yah just tell meh, "tuff titty."
Ma cloe's on meh. Yah jus rip meh offa yah
but I don't lose nothin' wen dismantl'd. Ma wangs
livin' wid alla dah secrets. What'cha hidin', sistah?
All ma life, I thout us as women
dat yah need'd meh like dah flo'
need ma wangs.
Need wood or yessirdays body
mudflaps owt yah cloe's
clean'd an' warsh'd real good.

My wangs are fly an' dah cleanes'
thangs alive
no fabric lef
dat can replace meh, cuz I'm on dah flo'
act like taday wuz yessirday
let's be fly. You and meh wid dese wangs

washin'board clean, offa dah flo'
alive! Not hangin' like dri'd up yessirdays
wen us cloe's all got wangs.

Aunt Fenny
She created everything with her fingers
mainly in the kitchen. Whipping up colors—
pinks, blues, and yellows.
When I visited,
I played God: A woman.
Colored in water
paint embedded in our skin
and clay caked under our nails.

I witness the cohesion
of clay—the gummy color of ecru
and ash—and knuckles,
maneuvering perspective
into parts.

My god,
is a woman
inferior?

I picture her sculpting
various hands
cut off at the wrist
mounted around the house
on shelves
like wisdom marinating for centuries.

My grandmama says, "She always made art.
It was something
about her fingers,
they would take funny shapes,
and you got 'em, too."

Rapper

If I were a rapper, I would have game
swagger
tongue hanging, just stepping into my verses,
strings swinging, hide, go getting,
spitting a cappella making it rain
your brain would lose its mind
I would spit flames
isolated firearms
pop-locking from the bang, the boom
of me dropping bombs
landmines on minds
I wouldn't mind blowing minds
I would blow up before time could tell
or mime with its hands
I wouldn't give a damn
I would be a jerk

Make your body jerk from jerking
skeeting that word flow
I would be MC Lyte lift your feet up
beat the beat up take care of all of mine,
no deadbeat
the knock crawling up your back
ma-mak-making you skip tracks
microphone check her
Woody pecker sounding like
Ahhhh, Ooo Ooo Ooo Ooo Ooo
Uhh!

Do you feel me?

Let you feel me if I were a rapper
I would be nasty
make you come

make you cum
run   wax off and on eardrums
fly! Wife my thoughts up
sending her on trips in my oblongata
sailing through skies
nine clouds bumping into mazes
spending nights and days in my brain
she would say, "Wow, you're amazing"
because I would be poking, stroking, provoking
verbs to get down
and dirty with my nouns
my spoken words would be smoking
words

Caught up behind bars
talking about how intricate their sentence is
rehearse lines, reverse minds back into time
when they first found out what art was
but I'm that artist
that's heartless
cause I don't know where my heart is
so regardless of what's going on
I spit!
spit up, regurgitate phrases on sheets
twisting 'em up
playing hand games
"Tweet-a-leet a-leet"
flipping up a birdie
signing its way out of cages

If I were a rapper,
I would be louder than one mic
with ten fucking stages!

If I were a rapper my heart wouldn't be

falling on these pages
falling into a world
clicking my shoes
three million times to stay afloat
only leaves me with red heels
no clues
why wanting to be home leaves me with
ashes and dust on my feet
walking around streets of my notepad
with a bottle of blues stumbling over my lines
trying to find my way
with no direction
working, erasing, scrubbing these sheets
trying to get rid of dirt
hurt is what I'm still seeing
I'm Emceeding
planting
dwelling in poet-trees
we need our own home
sanctuary, flowing off the dome
living by words, cause nobody
wants to be alone
so when life says no, I flow
heart beating out of chest
I say yes to the beat
in the background where
I can live through my words

Message
The Blues crowns the struggle
skies hold birds
the streets know wordsmiths, measurements,
herbalists, teachers
and they all got the news

"Be yourself
caged bird. Be yourself,"
they all chant, different hues of trauma
the brave hunts you down trying to ketchup
to the song like harp for Saul

The law! The law!

"Be yourself
caged bird. Be yourself,"
they all chant.
Our nation is still calculating
the right amount of people to grant
liberty and justice

For all! For all!

How many hands up before there's peace?
How many pulses lost? How much blood
pouring into congregations, clubs, and streets
full of birds?
Message!
They all chant, "Be yourself! Be yourself!"
Can'ts are coming and shooting
stars are amongst
the messengers running
quick!
fly, cover, recover

the wings flutter
freedom rings like air passing
when you hum that one song
when you sing that one song
that keeps you flying
freedom is singing, caged bird

soft and swift as your wings
bullets bellow baselines
and we sing, "We Shall Overcome."

We groove! And shall not be moved
the rhythm sounds like spiritual's
hieroglyphics underneath
tracking the progress. Are we there yet?
The Fearlessness in the cage
Do birds sing when afraid?
Do they?
Do birds run out of breath from flying?
I'm trying to figure it out but
"We've got to Move."
The cage is full of dreams and
"We've got to Move," they all chant.
And they all got the news
sirens and horns revealing the breakthrough
these songs, these wings are miracles
capping canopies, prayers
peeling layers
in loving memories
lighters, feathers flock to see you fly
Message!

What year is this?
The violence, boycotts, marching
the aggression boxing birds

into societal norms
big brother's watching

"Reform! Reform!"

The news sounds like battlefields
and we all got the news
the station the static.
Is that you in the attic
playing magical chairs?
Praising in the name of liberation?
Caged bird, there's a show on
the news and we all got it
oh my God, we all got it.
Caged bird   fly

and I don't know why
that's important but we all need to hear you
sing